WAGES, PR PROF IN THE 21ST CENTURY

An Introduction to Marx' Key Ideas on Waged Labour and Capitalism

PHILLIP SUTTON

With thanks for your help and guidance:

MH
S
MB
SJ
C
ER

Contents

Introduction   2

Section 1   6

1   Marx's approach to understanding   7
        the World Economy
2   Profit and Loss   8
3   Money, Price, Exchange Value and Use Value   9
4   Profit and the Process of Buying and Selling   12
5   Profit and Waged Labour   13
6   Labour and Labour Power   17
7   Commodities are Traded at Value   26
8   Capital and Capitalism   22
9   Surplus Value and the Accumulation of Capital   23

Section 2   25

10   The State and State Spending   26
11   The State and the Social Wage   28
12   Credit and Future debt   30
13   Wages and Productivity   32
14   Labour and the Standard of Living   34
15   Labour and Subsistence Wage   37
16   The Different Parts into which Unpaid Labour
        can be broken down   40
17   Wages and Inflation   42
18   In Conclusion   44

Footnotes   46

Introduction

I am writing this pamphlet not to present myself as an expert in Marx and his writings, I most clearly am not, but to focus on what is important in Marx's analysis related to some very basic questions about the exploitation of the working class. To explain these ideas is still important for workers today. In fact, it is arguable that a return to basics is even more important as the workers movement is far smaller and less influential than it was in the 19th century and capitalism has somehow managed to strengthen the argument that capitalism is eternal, that wages are normal, that money, wealth and poverty are just what happens and that waged labour doesn't need to be understood, it just is. Capitalism has been around so long it is presented as the peak of civilisation.

Part of what I want to address in this pamphlet is that society has changed so significantly since the time Marx wrote 'Wages, Price and Profit' that there are many new issues that need further explanation. My purposes are therefore to explain the main concepts of Marx's work as well as discuss these new factors that have emerged and how they affect workers today.

In Section 1 of the pamphlet, I intend to go back to basics of how capitalism works with regard to labour and how it generates profit and in Section 2 to address changes in capitalist society since Marx's day that relate to the exploitation of labour and also to look at some of the myths and misunderstandings that capitalism uses in today's society to try to justify itself and prevent us understanding what capitalism does to us. This means that, whilst I am clearly using Marx's writing and ideas as a source and a framework, I do not intend to revisit all sections of his book but rather to focus on the major elements of his writings that are relevant to workers today and to present this in modern language so that it is more accessible to readers in the 21st Century.

With this in mind, this pamphlet will not attempt to make an all-embracing analysis of capitalist society. I do not intend to discuss any of the various theories relating to capitalism's social and political history nor its crises nor even the history of class struggle. The focus is purely on what relates to work and to waged labour.

Marx's original pamphlet, 'Wages Prices and Profit', was in fact based on a speech by Karl Marx given to the General Council of the First International in

1865 and was intended to argue against the views of J Weston who was in favour of restricting workers wages.[i]

To do this Marx had to explain the wage system and how it upheld capitalism. While it was written therefore to answer specific questions it clearly developed to form what I have always seen as one of the 2 most important writings on capitalism's economics. The other is "What is Economics" by Rosa Luxemburg. Both of these documents address a range of basic issues that define what capitalism is - without expecting the reader to be or become an economist. Luxemburg had the advantages of being an economics lecturer and a very good writer. Marx on the other hand came up with extremely important ideas but not only wrote in a language which is not very clear for 21st century readers but also tended to analyse topics very deeply in a way that is not so relevant to readers today.

What was life like in the mid-1800s when Marx was writing? Well don't forget this is the time of the horse and cart, of cobbles and mud roads and of the poorhouse. Some roads had gas lighting but there were no electric supplies to individual houses and, what is more, no water or sewerage systems. Flushing toilets in separate rooms were the preserve of the super rich as was gas lighting. Cooking was by wood or coal burning ranges which would be the source of hot water too. Workers in industrial towns generally lived in back to back housing which frequently had only 2 rooms (one up one down) little lighting and limited outside washing and toilet facilities. Income tax was paid in the UK but only by those earning over £150 per year (average wage for a labourer at that time was about £50 per year and an engineer about £100 per year) and National Insurance systems to provide social benefits in the UK were non-existent. Interesting to note here that Germany developed private social insurance systems earlier than the UK because the German state spent less on social welfare than the UK did on poorhouse relief!

Workers paid rent but had no service bills, no income tax or national insurance, no welfare benefits and little in the way of protective legislation (only in legislation of 1832 did child labour become restricted to a max of 12 hours per day and 48 hours per week - for children under 13 that is. Children between 13 and 18 years could be asked to work up to 69 hours per week!)

In Marx's time, capitalism was only just becoming dominant in society so the experience of a wage-based system was very limited. Capitalism was a relatively newly formed system with pretensions to create individual freedom so, for me, this explains why he had to delve into his material in such depth to explain how the various elements of capitalism worked.

Nowadays, we have had a great deal more experience of wages, credit systems, currency rates, inflation etc and therefore workers can have a much better idea of just what capitalism is and how it works.

Luxemburg addresses the distinction between capitalism and the way feudal society worked in 'What is Economics?' She pointed to the fact that Feudalism did not have economics or accounting systems in the current sense of the words because both the king and the serf were only concerned with whether they possessed enough goods for their own purposes rather than the value of what they possessed. The ruling class simply recorded all the assets they owned – and they owned everything (eg the Domesday Book assessed all lands and resources to give William the Conqueror a more accurate basis for taxation and redistribution purposes). The serfs made what they needed for themselves and bought only a few essentials and the ruling class of the time owned everything and collected their subsistence from the serfs. Within capitalism however, the system is based on goods being produced for sale on a mass market that neither workers nor capitalists can control.

On capitalism, Luxemburg wrote:

"Today we know no master, no slaves, no feudal lords, no bondsmen. Liberty and equality before the law have removed all despotic relations....". She goes on to add "... today a private enterprise, even the most gigantic, is only a fragment of the great economic structure which embraces the entire globe – while these units are disciplined to the utmost, the entity of all the so-called national economics, ie the world economy, is completely unorganised. In the entity which embraces oceans and continents, there is not planning, no consciousness, no regulation, only the blind clash of unknown, unrestrained forces playing a capricious game with the economic destiny of man. ... the form which this sovereignty of capital takes is not despotism but anarchy."[ii]

Marx made it clear that although under capitalism workers appear to be paid for the whole of their labour, in reality they are only paid for a part and the surplus is actually an unpaid contribution to the wealth being accumulated by capitalists. Workers appear to have gained legal freedom as individuals in society but in reality remain slaves to an exploitative wage system. In 'Wages, Prices and Profits' he focuses on the real conditions of labour and these discoveries are still valid today.

If anything there is less effort today to really investigate and understand how capitalism works. This is mostly because the fake socialist and communists submerge Marx's ideas in a cauldron of myths and confusions. They present their misunderstandings and total distortions of Marx's theories to justify their positions of power within today's capitalism. These fakers present the state's power within capitalism as a form of socialism and a benefit for the working class and then even justify the perpetuation of wage labour as somehow socialist in content.

SECTION 1

This section contains explanations of the analyses that Marx made showing how capitalism functions to produce new value, accumulate new capital and exploit workers.

1   Marx's approach to understanding the world economy

It is not possible to understand how the economy works from looking at the businesses run by Branson, Gates or Bezos nor even from the policies of any politicians like Corbyn or Johnson or Trump. Similarly, you cannot work out what an elephant is by first looking at every piece of skin, bone, muscle, hair separately. Rather you must look at the whole first then interpret the physiology and actions of all those components in the context of the whole. The same is true with a social and economic system. You cannot learn what capitalism is from looking at the behaviour of individuals and individual businesses. To understand how today's world system works you need to look at the whole and generalise (ie reduce to basics) the behaviours you see. Only with this approach, can you understand how individual elements fit into the overall pattern and how they can be analysed.

In fact in the world of business you will find that firms function differently from one another even if they are making the same products. Firms may have common features in terms of product, equipment and or departments but each firm establishes its own internal structure, job roles and even its own language and abbreviations (for people who work elsewhere, this is always a point of annoyance and confusion but all industries and often individual firms develop their own language and abbreviations to simplify internal discussion). More importantly firms develop their own software and documentation and hence their own processes to manage production.

Capitalism cannot be understood therefore from analysing a single firm. It can only be understood by looking at the whole and then generalising the processes involved. There is just too much detail in a world as big as capitalism has become, so generalising fundamentally means identifying the common features and the standard behaviours in the processes and relationships that comprise the system. This is not always quantifiable but the quality of the generalisation can be tested. How do you know that a generalisation is valid, well, you have to keep checking the understanding against events in reality and assessing validity and, when necessary, making adjustments. Remember Marx did not come up with his overall view of capitalism without many years of investigation.

2   Profit and Loss

It will be useful first of all to explain the key terms that are used in the accounts of capitalist firms. These terms have come to be used in everyday language so it is worth knowing what they actually mean.

Costs or expenses are incurred by businesses and amongst them are wages and salaries, the material content of the products, factory maintenance, services, insurances, marketing and so forth. The costs of these elements of running a business are totalled and presented in business accounts as the total costs that have been incurred over a specific period.

The other main element of these accounts is the figure for total sales or income. This is produced by totalling all sales values of all the business' products over the same period of time as the costs.

Profit is therefore simply sales value minus total costs in that same period. If the sales figure is greater than the costs then a profit is made, if costs is higher than the sales value then a loss has been made by a business during that period.

The profit that has been identified is a significant indicator that the business is worthwhile, it is an indicator of performance.

The value of a business is basically the total of the value of its buildings, machinery, stock, money in the bank, creditors and debtors, otherwise known as the firm's assets.

It is instructive therefore to recognise then that the terms and concepts used by capitalism in analysing business performance are drawn from a specific point of view ie the needs of the businesses within the system.

The perspective changes when we look at capitalism as a whole so we need to differentiate Marx's terms and concepts to understand the generalised processes he identified.

3   Money, Price, Exchange Value and Use Value

In investigating capitalism, Marx realised that capitalism's terminology was insufficient for explaining the real processes at work and that new definitions were needed. Some of his theory was developed from the ideas of earlier theoreticians but Marx was able to draw them together to differentiate his global understanding from the terms and concepts used by individual firms. In this chapter we will look specifically at his key terms – use value, exchange value, price and money.

Use Value

All goods have an exchange value and a use value. Let us first consider what is the use value. It is not an everyday term today but clearly any item or service that is for sale must have some use to the purchaser otherwise it just wouldn't be bought. In the case of status objects such as works of art and house decorations, that use value may just be its rarity or its value as an investment whereas a decoration, on the other hand, its use is simply being attractive. However, by and large, most use values are related to some physical task the item will carry out for the owner.

Use value does not have an actual value therefore in strict monetary terms, it has a social value for the owner. This may sound odd in the sense that the owner pays money for an item to obtain its use value. Consider though the value of bread, milk or baked beans and so forth. Their price is low but they are considered essentials in terms of our subsistence and hence have a high use value whereas caviar would have a high price but its use value is relatively small. Spectacles can be an essential item also but whose prices can vary from very high as in designer products to very low as everyday wear yet their use value must be the same in both cases. So use value can vary and is not the same as purchase price.

Exchange Value and Price

Let us now move onto exchange value. We have learnt that the products that you buy have a use value that is fixed against social needs at any given time (in other words the use values of items and services may change over time and in different locations) and mean the item is worth purchasing at a given price.

That purchase price is what Marx termed the exchange value. This emphasises that all buying and selling is an exchange on a marketplace.

Inflation, location, sales method, and even customer type can impact on price to make it higher or lower even though the product's use value remains the same. For example, a hand mangle had a high use value up to the 1950s but since then electrical machines have replaced them in social use and hence eliminated their use value - at least in countries with a reliable electrical supply. In under-developed regions of the world a hand mangle would still today have a high use value but an electrical washing machine could have no use value at all, particularly in rural areas. Clearly though a manufacturer would not be willing to give away a product with no use value, it would still have a sales price attached to it even if the customer needed to additionally buy an expensive generator to make use of it. Indeed, in such a situation, its position as a status item could well drive its sales price higher than average.

Overall there is no simple relationship between exchange value and use value. From the above examples, exchange value and use value can both vary independently and without any physical variation in the item itself. What must be understood therefore is that exchange value is not a representation of some inherent worth, it also is socially determined by its position in a market place.

The exchange value of any item is therefore socially determined and is essentially an average of all prices of that item on the marketplace.   There is no real possibility of calculating that exchange value precisely because it is an average of a very complex set of factors. This idea is developed and explained further in the Chapter on Labour and Labour Power.

In summary, exchange value varies because in different locations, conditions and times, the price or exchange value of any given product will change. Inflation is one item that acts as proof of this statement as it has become a permanent concern in the world economy and clearly shows that the price of a good will increase over time at varying rates in different locations. Also, competition between firms can also drive the prices of some products down even after inflation. Price is therefore not a statement of the real or internal value of an item. Price is its value on the existing market. We buy products because they have use value for us as individuals. We buy products at an exchange value which is determined by social and economic interaction of all products. The price we pay is simply the current estimation of that exchange value.

Money

Once upon a time money represented value because coins were made of metal to the face value on the coin. Also bank notes were genuine promissory notes which could be changed into precious metal on demand. At that time therefore money had an actual exchange value.

Today, in the 21st Century, coins and bank notes are simply a means of exchange in an increasingly complex economy. They have no intrinsic value as metal or paper, a fact that is recognised in this electronic age by the storage of our money in electronic bank accounts where there is no physical element at all, just an electronic record on a computer file. What money does have, whether appearing as notes, coins or electronic data, is a use value as a method of exchange.

This is a social value and continues only in as much as people trust banks and government to honour this use value. Once doubt creeps in about the viability of a bank or of a government system then this is when we start to see runs on a bank where people try to get their own money out - only to find out that it isn't there. When people are not able to obtain their own money in this way, its use value as a means of exchange has disappeared and banks will not supply the money. Banks do not hold the full value in cash that the bank statements identify. Similarly governments cannot pay the value of the money they have issued and, if trust in the money market goes, then the exchange value of their currency drops and price inflation increases.

Coins and banknotes therefore have no actual value that equates to the face value they are given, but, they have a use value as a means of exchange which is convenient to handle and to store for future use. One noteworthy additional use value is that currency can be used in accounting records for businesses and in economics analysis of the world system.

4   Profits and the Process of Buying and Selling

In the world of the capitalist, it is believed that it is the process of good management that makes profits. In particular, profits are earned by the selling of goods and services at a high price and the buying of goods at low prices. This may be true at the level of the individual business but it just cannot be true at the level of global capital.

If we could take a snapshot of global capital as a whole we would see a definite quantity of all assets in existence and we could work out a total value for them all. Easier said than done but it must be true.   If then we assume that a specific product has a certain value within that accumulated global capital but has been sold by one capitalist to another at an exchange value higher than this value, the seller may indeed be said to have a profit. However, what of the position of the buyer who now has a product that cost a figure higher than its actual value – the buyer has made a loss equal to the seller's profit. This of course works the other way round too. If the seller sells at below the exchange value, then the seller has made a loss and the buyer has made a profit.

So overall, what benefit is there for global capital from buying and selling? None. The profit made by one trading partner equals the loss made by the other. The result is simply a redistribution of wealth.

What Marx established is that what a capitalist sees as a profit for him or herself is not at all a profit for global capital. Buying and selling is a completely neutral activity that only shifts value around in society. It does not generate new value.

It is for this reason that the capitalist cannot understand the real world and the position of the working class within it. Capitalists see only their individual role in society and its consequences for themselves.

5 Profit and Waged Labour

So now we come to the most important question to be asked: just how is new value created?

The capitalist pays workers a wage for the work they do. From the perspective of the capitalists, they are simply buying labour and hence paying a price for it. This viewpoint means labour is simply another commodity and the wage is simply the exchange value of that labour.

But we already know from the last chapter that buying and selling does not create new value, so what other action takes place that can create value? The only activity that is left that can activate this creation of value is the actual work done by labour – as distinct from the purchase of that labour.

Looking at the world economy as a whole, we see the economy consists, at core, of raw materials, premises, machinery, transportation systems, office and management systems, market systems for buying and selling goods and of course labour. Now of that list raw materials, premises, machinery, transportation systems, office and management systems have a physical existence and a cost to businesses, but on their own they conduct no activity. To put it bluntly, they just sit around waiting for something to happen. In themselves they can do nothing to create new products. These are all the inactive material elements that act as inputs into the manufacturing process.

So once businesses own or have set up these items, from that point on workers are required to administer the firm, operate the machinery and process the raw materials into finished goods. Wages may be the cost of labour to the manufacturer, but in employing workers capitalists are able to turn this lists of costs (including the wages themselves) into sales products that have a higher total value. In this way capitalists gain their profit.

This then is the simple key to the whole problem of what creates new value; it is the labour process. Labour power is a commodity that has special properties; it creates new value.

This recognition is the starting point for anyone who is trying to understand how capitalism really works.

Labour converts premises, machinery and raw materials from individual components into a finished good of far greater value than those original components and it is the application of labour that achieves this. Most workers know this from their own personal experience although admittedly it is clearer in some processes than others. The waged bricklayer working in a gang is fully aware of how much is paid and how many bricks can be laid in a specific time. That bricklayer will also be aware that the gangmaster who employs the bricklayer earns a payment from the building firm dependant on the total bricks laid. It is relatively easy to calculate how much profit that gangmaster makes from the labour costs that turn bricks and mortar supplied by the building firm into walls for buildings. If the gangmaster didn't make a profit from that labour, he would not be employing that labour, he probably would be in a different business entirely

Until the latter half of the 20th Century it was more normal for manufacturing of a product to take place on one large site. Manufacturers undertook the manufacturing of components and the supply of related services inhouse. It is of course far less clear to the individual worker how his or her work generates new value in a large scale enterprise with a more complex manufacturing processes but it is still the case that the accumulation of work tasks undertaken by workers in a single firm leads to a completed finished product that is ready for sale on a marketplace, whether this is a car, a TV or a computer and so on. That completed product once sold generates new value to which all workers in the firm have contributed.

Manufacturing today has changed in structure though and it is far more common for firms to operate with a long supply chain where the supply of components and services are outsourced to other firms. This is just an adjustment in how capitalism finds it more profitable to organise manufacturing. Today manufacturing techniques, electronic communication systems and cheap transportation mean that is far more common for finished goods to be put together from a range of sub-assemblies prepared at different sites. Global, national and even local firms will use outsourced supplies as a way of limiting costs and enabling them to focus on key areas in their business.

This makes no difference to global capitalism; each stage of the supply chain generates its own portion of value which contributes to the final market value and the global accumulation of new value.

This is not only true for manufacturing but also for raw materials processing and agriculture. The land must be rented or purchased of course but from that stage on, the processing of extracted raw materials requires workers and machines (whose construction required other workers). So for example iron ore may be in the ground freely available but its processing requires it to be brought to the surface and processed by labourers, geologists, surveyors, labourers, chemists and engineers and of course machinery built by other workers. The labour power of all these processes is incorporated into a market value for unprocessed iron ore and, after processing, for the exchange value of the finished steel. Agriculture equally requires labourers, machine operators, distributors and presumably chemists too who all contribute to the cost of the food we buy in shops.

A further complication in manufacturing today is the use of robotic machinery.

Some argue that these robots mean society can go on expanding and eliminate the need for work and indeed workers. They are correct to imply that robotics have and will have an impact on social life just as in the past the emergence of large scale factories changed the way people lived to service these factories. They suggest though that capitalism can become a leisure society that has robots doing all the work!! Such fantasy! It is clear from history that this just does not happen. When technology develops and reduces the need of labour in specific areas of manufacturing, then one or more of a variety of consequences come about – either production increases and working hours remain the same; or manufacturing finds new products using that technology; or finally labour increases in the manufacture of industrial machinery that designs and creates the equipment that uses the new technology. Yes, we have seen overall unemployment rise and fall at local, national and global levels with the invention and application of new technologies (an impact which can be extremely brutal on those affected) but at no point have we seen these dreams of a leisure society become reality.

Workers can see from their own experiences that new technology may disrupt and change the type of work that they do, but they continue to have to work just as hard if not harder than previously.

So new technology and, more specifically, robots do not alter the basic concept, they just change the precise process of manufacture and profit generation. What's more, computer controlled machinery, ie robots and communications systems, is still just machinery which has been manufactured by software designers, computer designers, computer assemblers and installation engineers and its actual operation still has to been overseen by engineers. So computerisation and robotics do not eliminate labour, they simply reduce direct labour on the final stages and take the waged labour back to previous stages of the manufacturing process.

To repeat, in terms of the value of global capital, extra value is created at each stage of production and assembly, so that even a totally robotised manufacturing process at the final stage, will contribute to the accumulation for global capital from every stage of the manufacturing process. In Chapter 8 we will see Marx's formula for how this capital accumulation works.

6   Labour and Labour Power

We have established in Chapter 5 that because the capitalist pays a purchase price for labour, it is a commodity that has in fact a special characteristic, its use creates new value over and above the wages the workers earn. So much is clear. We now need to establish more precisely how this works in practice.

This is one of the more difficult concepts to grasp in Marx's analysis of capitalism.

From the point of view of the capitalist, it would seem obvious that the price or value of labour is simply the cost of employing a worker and that the finished good is sold at a price above its cost so that a profit can be made. This suggests that workers are paid for the work done. This cannot be the case however. Remember, the buying and selling of commodities at their exchange value, no matter what they are, does not generate profits for the system as a whole.

What actually happens in practice is that the wage, the exchange value of labour, is determined by contracts made prior to actually doing the work. What workers are paid for therefore is not the work they actually do or have done, but their power to labour; they commit themselves to working for a specific sum of money over a specific number of hours per week and the capitalist pays a pre-determined price for this. Even piecework jobs fit this pattern too.

For capitalists to make a profit out of the work done and its pre-determined cost, workers can only be receiving part of the additional value that their labour creates.

From the perspective of the working class then, what we see from the analysis of the creation of additional value is that, for the period of labour that workers provide, they are paid for only a part of their labour and the capitalist takes possession of the remainder of their labour. The capitalist receives this as unpaid labour

When the working class sells its labour power then, this is what provides the basis for the growth of the capital owned by the ruling class. It is the only active element in the manufacturing and distribution system that isn't simply a 'buying and selling' process and hence it is the labour process that creates new wealth.

It would seem obvious now to ask how do we work out the value of labour and the additional value produced but there is a problem and I would suggest it to be impossible to calculate the value of labour power as an accurate figure. It is the logical conclusion of Marx's premises that new value comes from the labour process but whilst we can see the price that the employer pays, to work out the actual value of labour would require looking at all wages, all wages in the same sector or job, all support wages, all costs and wages of component supply and raw materials supply, all social wages costs and probably all unproductive labour costs as well as the value of all production. This would really be next to impossible to even estimate.

It may be thought that this demolishes Marx's analysis but in fact if you look at the actual wage that the employer pays, you can ask the same question, how is that price of labour determined, and you would have the same problem. There is no calculation possible.

Both of these values are, in practice, socially fixed over time by experience of what makes a profit or not and experience of the operation of the market. If it doesn't work out well financially for the capitalist, then either the wage or work process or the sales price gets changed. Let's be clear, Capitalism is not a system of conscious control, it is an anarchic system of markets where nobody is actually in control of what really happens.

To complete this section, let us analyse the waged labour transaction again. The exchange value or price of labour is what workers sell their own labour power at, so for example let's assume the worker is selling labour power at £400 for a 40 hour working week. The nature of the labour transaction is that capitalism gains over and above the payment it makes for that labour. Labour creates new value but it doesn't get paid the full value of what it creates.

This means that workers effectively only do paid work for part of the week and so, as an example, the actual value to the employers of the first 20 hours work done in the week could be the entire £400 that is paid to workers. In the second part of the week the workers is in effect unpaid and the employer benefits by obtaining goods worth a further £400 from the next 20 hours. Overall, the worker receives a payment of only part of the value of the product they produced whilst the employer obtains finished goods worth £400 above what was paid for components, manufacturing costs. This is the surplus value generated by the labour process.

These figures are just an example. However if we compare the total annual wages in the UK which is approx £0.88 trillion[iii] (for all incomes including management and even overpaid footballers) and the annual GDP at £2 trillion then you can see that, in fact, they are more likely to be an underestimation of overall value gained by employers.

7 Commodities are Traded at Value

From previous chapters we have recognised that the buying and selling of goods on a market cannot create a profit for global capital. This itself suggests that commodities are traded at their real value, however there are other implications of this knowledge that we should recognise.

Firstly, we know that workers in general therefore only receive part of the value of the labour they provide.   Therefore, the real value of labour is the total of the paid and unpaid labour. It is the full or real value of labour that establishes the value of the finished good rather than the exchange cost of that labour.

Consequently, the exchange value of finished goods is totalled from the cost of using the fixed assets, the cost of all components and the full or real value of the labour (ie the total value of the paid and unpaid portions of labour) expended to produce them.

This has an important consequence, for as Marx stresses, the capitalist:

"... sells not only what has cost him an equivalent, but he sells also what has cost him nothing, although it has cost his workman labour. The cost of the commodity to the capitalist and its real cost are different things. I repeat, therefore, that normal and average profits are made by selling commodities not *above*, but *at their real values.*"[iv]

Having established this important fact about the exchange value of goods, we must nevertheless also recognise that the exchange value, the market value of goods, is not fixed but does indeed vary.   These variations however are the product of market fluctuations and not wage related factors. Wage inflation is a common way of blaming workers for economic problems but remember that workers are actually underpaid for their work done.   Inflation is an example where all exchange value varies as a result mainly of over-expenditure by governments.

The other well-known element of price variation is supply and demand. Capitalists like to be able to blame supply and demand particularly if they make losses. However we have now seen that goods sell at their real value so supply and demand does not actually fix that value but rather it just causes the temporary fluctuations in price above and below the real value of goods.

Again Marx explains:

"At the moment when supply and demand equilibrate each other, and therefore cease to act, the *market price* of a commodity coincides with its *real value*, with the standard price round which its market prices oscillate. In inquiring into the nature of that VALUE, we have therefore nothing at all to do with the temporary effects on market prices of supply and demand. The same holds true of wages and of the prices of all other commodities." [v]

The Labour Theory of Value

The consequence of the recognition that the sale of commodities takes place at their real value and that that exchange value of commodities is related to the value of the total labour that went into producing the commodities lead Marx to what is called the Labour Theory of Value. It was not his discovery as such but was adapted from ideas presented by earlier economists.

"The labour theory of value is the proposition that the value of a commodity is equal to the quantity of socially necessary labour-time required for its production".[vi]

The term socially necessary labour time is used because it is not a calculation that a capitalist can perform. Marx used the term to describe this situation where the exchange value of commodities is established socially, ie in practice in the real world, from the accumulated labour time spent (paid and unpaid) on all the raw materials, components and final assembly of commodities.

8   Capital and Capitalism

Before going further there are terms we have to make clearer. Marx used the term 'Capital' to denote all physical assets and money too that had been and would be used in the manufacturing process to create new or replacement products ie new 'Capital'.

Because production keeps creating new value in this continuous process, it means that the amount of capital in existence is continually growing. This is what Marx referred to as the 'Accumulation of Capital'.

Hence the term capitalism itself comes from the recognition that our current economic system has the creation and recreation of capital, ie new assets, at the core of the system. It is a system that depends on continual growth and its only real purpose is to expand capital.   Its management is no longer operated by birthright or cultural rules but by ownership of assets and their use to create and expand wealth.   As a system, it is extremely dynamic and able to grow at a far greater rate than previous economic systems.   In this system of wage labour and production of commodities for sale on a market, for workers and capitalists alike, the product itself is effectively irrelevant.   To workers it is irrelevant what they work on, they just need to earn an income to survive.   For capitalists, if they don't achieve growth or profit, either the firm will be bankrupted by competition from other firms or the product they are producing will be abandoned and something else produced.

Marx divided components of the manufacturing process into constant capital and variable capital.   Because his purpose was not to investigate the process within a firm but that of the world as a whole, he needed to categorise assets in a different way to represent the fact that labour produces all assets.   Marx used the term constant capital to include all raw materials, machinery, premises and all service, administration and financial costs.   The term variable capital was used to denote all labour costs incurred in the production process and the cost of maintenance of that work force which means not just the actual labour costs but also the range of social wage or the support services that are provided to maintain that labour ie education, health service, pensions etc.   This value must also include the cost of supporting family so ultimately includes the cost of the reproduction of the working class as well.

9   Surplus Value and The Accumulation of Capital

In previous chapters we have discussed the relationship between waged labour, the range of costs incurred and the employer's profit. As we have seen, profit and loss accounts explain how an individual employer or business makes a profit, but they do not explain how wealth is created for global capitalism.

In generalising and taking capitalism as whole, Marx was investigating the components of existing wealth and their function and, as we have seen in the previous chapter, established constant capital and variable capital as the 2 main types of asset. From Marx's perspective there was no point in identifying raw materials and components separate to the fixed assets as undertaken in individual business accounts and Marx kept labour and the reproduction of labour as a separate item in his analysis because of its key role in creating and accumulating new value.

At this point we need to introduce another simplification – the production cycle. Clearly, production by all firms is randomly organised but it helps the analysis of the world economy to think of production taking place in a production cycle in a specific period of say 1 year (but it could just as easily be 1 decade or 1 month).

The model that Marx discovered represents the process that capitalism as a whole goes through in that cycle and breaks down the different elements of how capital accumulates.   It is a snapshot of the elements of value in the capital that has been accumulated up to that point in time. This model is:

$c + v + sv = $ Total Capital.

Where

c =   Constant Capital existing at the start of the cycle
v =   Variable Capital which is the labour cost during the cycle
sv =   Surplus Value, the additional value generated by the production cycle

Total capital = Total value of capital at the end of a cycle and ready for the next cycle

It is worth noting here that Marx's term in his native German for surplus value was 'Mehrwert' which translates better as added value or additional value and this is perhaps clearer than the term surplus value which has become established in English

Remember also, this formula only works properly at the level of total capital because all manufacturers work at their own pace and in their own time, so its far more anarchic than this simplified model would suggest.

At the end of this hypothetical production cycle the total value of all capital accumulated and ready for the next production cycle is the sum of:

c   which is the value of the machinery and other physical resources and the value of the components and raw materials that has been used during the cycle.

v   is the value of the labour to process c and generate new value in the form of new products and goods for the market. This includes the cost of labour to each capitalist of course but also includes the value of the social wage that the working class receives from the state and to some extent from employers. The value of the end products of this cycle must therefore include the cost of the entire variable capital.

sv   is the value of the unpaid labour that the capitalist obtains from the worker class during the labour process and which represents the new value that has been created and contributes to the accumulation of new capital.

This is clearly a simplification of the real world. It does not identify the availability of money to maintain that cycle nor the exact form of physical or financial capital nor political or legal issues nor any detail of how the market functions within capitalism. It does not need to! It is a model that works to explain how the economy of capitalism grows and how accumulated capital is developed and contributes to new cycles of production.

SECTION 2

This section looks at the main ways in which capitalism has changed since Marx's time. This is not intended to be a comprehensive analysis of capitalism today but highlights some specific new features and myths that have emerged in the last 150 years and which affect workers and the wage system.

10   The State and State Spending

Probably the most significant change in the economy since Marx's time is the growth of the nation state and how it manages society. In the mid 19th century the nation state was only just becoming important in establishing the rules, regulations and technical standards for how each national economy had to operate. One example of this in the UK is time standards; GMT was not adopted legally for the whole of the UK until 1880. Nevertheless the railway network had been using it since 1847 whilst the rest of the UK was still using Local Mean Time – which meant every town on different longitudes had different times!! The state at this time was still a relatively small institution comprising primarily royalty, parliament and armed forces with little in the way of administrative apparatus.

Figure 1. Central Government Expenditure as % of GDP [vii]

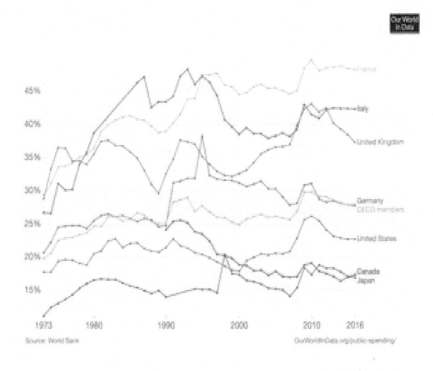

Nowadays, in the 21st century, the state has become the major employer and the most important single institution in every major nation of the world. As can be seen from Fig.1 even in the USA, supposedly a bastion of the free market, the government spends the equivalent of nearly 30% of the nation's GDP. The level in the UK is only just over 40%. There are countries with low state expenditure but most of them do tend to be small countries with minor economies.

Does the state create wealth? No, it may print money when its needed for circulation purposes, but generally speaking it controls society to ensure capitalism functions well (and keeps the working class creating wealth for the ruling class). As Marx and Engels identified, it has the primary role of managing classes in society - in favour of the ruling class of course. To some extent the policies and legislation produced by the nation state can act as a stimulus by creating more effective economic conditions for businesses to function in. The state absorbs money from the economy through taxation in order to pay for a vast administrative and decision-making apparatus as will institutions for social control such as the police and army, border controls and so forth. This type of expenditure does not contribute though towards the growth of capital in new cycles of production; from the global point of view, this spending is consequently primarily waste expenditure.

Many states do own and manage nationalised industries, or at least have gone through a period of doing so, and certainly the state, in this role, undertakes productive manufacturing and creates surplus value.

The significance of these roles and its now comprehensive role in setting and administering legislation which manages the workforce in each nation, mean it has to be accepted that, whatever the level of state ownership, we live under a system of state capitalism.

Where there appears to be no little or no private capitalism, some states have maintained they are workers' states which run the society on behalf of the workers but this is just nonsense. It matters not a jot that workers work in a state enterprise or a private enterprise. When state workers are paid wages and the machinery they work on and the products of their labour are in the control of enterprises and nations that operate within a world market, this is still capitalist exploitation of the working class.

11   The State and the Social Wage

An important function of the state today lies in providing or arranging for benefits for the unemployed, young, elderly, poor and so forth. Education, Health and Care Services, Pensions, Public Transport, sickness and unemployment benefits are all supported wholly or partially by the state. This varies of course from nation to nation depending on local needs and resources. These services provided to workers whether by the state or, in some cases, by the employers themselves are termed the Social Wage. It is a wage that is not paid directly in cash but in services or benefits.

In Marx's time there was very little social wage contributed by the state but today it is a significant figure worldwide.   In 2018 the average of social wage expenditure for OECD countries relative to GDP is ca 20% and this rises to as much as 30% in France for example.

Figure 2. Public Social Spending as % of GDP [viii]

In Chapter 9 we discussed variable capital as the labour cost incurred by the capitalist. Certainly, in the early days of capitalism, this was simply the wage paid to the worker because they only had that sum to survive on and provide for all their needs. It had to be enough for the worker to provide for a family and support any children until they were old enough to strike out on their own and work to earn their own income. This variable capital includes therefore day-to-day subsistence as well as the reproduction and education costs of the workforce. The ruling class cannot just magic new workers into existence, it has to support this process. Reproduction of the workforce has therefore always been part of the capitalists' expenses.

In the 20th and 21st centuries we can see that the indirect maintenance of the workforce has gradually had to be taken over by the state because of the importance of supporting business in an ever more complex world and because it is far more efficient to provide these services from a central institution. It became a task that could no longer be left in its entirety to individual capitalists because the results of bad practice can be enormously negative for capitalism as a whole. Robert Owen and the Cadbury family were exceptions as 'enlightened' employers so it became a role for the state to try to head off the danger of workers' revolts.

More importantly though, who actually pays for this social wage?

The state gains its income from taxes and charges made on the workers' wages and on economic activity in the national economy. Out of this income the state pays the social wage as well as maintains the vast network with which the ruling class needs to support and protect itself, something which we have already identified as waste expenditure. The state takes wealth from workers and employers but it must leave enough both for workers' subsistence and for the surplus value that grows production; so the actual or original source of the state's income must be the unpaid labour that is taken from workers. The difference being that the social wage is part of surplus value that contributes to capital growth whereas the support for the state and the luxurious subsistence demanded by the ruling class is just waste as far as global capital is concerned.

In the end this process makes no difference to Marx's formula for global capital (see Chapter 9) but it does expose how complex these social systems have become today.

12   Credit and Future Debt

This issue was discussed by Marx but in less depth presumably because whilst there was significant debt in his time, it was primarily incurred by the state and the capitalists themselves. He only raised the issue as in the discussion of how surplus value is divided up (see Chapter 15), to show that the interest payments came out of the unpaid labour extracted by the capitalist. In fact, the reason that the level of commercial and state debt was relatively very high in the early 19th century was that the state drew little taxation on incomes. Income Tax only became a permanent source of funding for the UK government from 1842 onwards.

War played a significant part in creating national debt at the start of the 19th century and from 1915 onwards with the 2 world wars. However, credit mechanisms for household debt have come to the fore since the onset of the 20th Century when the nation state began to play a much bigger role in the management of the social economy.

From the latter part of the 20th century, debt is once again starting to increase significantly and, as a result of stagnating wages, UK household debt has now become a major burden on the working class.   This is no accident, in the UK Thatcher took a major step in this process by encouraging working class families to buy their own homes. Special rates were offered but it was clearly a step that would increase household debt levels and cement workers' dependence on their employers' interests. It appears to present a better lifestyle but for the working class it just means another ball and chain to carry. In the following period, it has also become far harder to open a saving account than obtain credit. This can only be a strategic decision by the state. The consequence is that in the first part of the 21st Century government total debt has increased to 2.5 times that of GDP and household debt lies between 90% to 110% of GDP[ix]

What does this level of debt mean?

Firstly and very importantly, it shows the capitalism can no longer generate the level of wealth to support itself and enrich its population. Capitalism now relies on a credit system to allow it to function economically. A healthy economic system would not need to depend on such large systems of credit.

Secondly, it means the working class is being even more closely tied into the capitalist system.   Not only are they dependent for wages, but now, with large debts from mortgages and cars and household furniture, future earnings are already spoken for and workers are less easily going to enter conflict with employers.

Indeed, nowadays in the UK, the need for credit has become so great, that new industries have arisen offering services to help manage an individual's credit status to make it easier to obtain even more loans. So important and widespread is the need for a good credit status, we are even being offered pre-application checks on loans to ensure that it is not affected by a failed application!

Finally let us remember that all credit, both for workers and for the capitalist, is a loan against future earnings. This can only mean greater risks in future.

Charles Dickens was not wrong in summarising capitalism's early ethical stance relating to financial behaviour.

"Annual income twenty pounds, annual expenditure nineteen six, result happiness. Annual income twenty pounds, annual expenditure twenty pound ought and six, result misery." [x]

13   Wages and Productivity

One of the major ways in which capitalism has managed to survive in the past century has been by increasing productivity.

It is only at the beginning of the 20th Century that capitalism began investigating and improving business strategies and management systems to increase efficiency. Beginning with Taylor's studies into 'Time and Motion' and pay, there have been contributions by a range of specialists in business and manufacturing practice until today when we have 'Total Quality Management' and 'Just in Time' systems that aim to improve productivity and efficiency in manufacture even further.   Increased productivity leads to greater profits for individual businesses and this competitive process on the market ultimately stimulates the overall expansion of capital as a whole.

Furthermore, the reinvestment of surplus value into fixed and variable capital leads to the advancement of technology in the productive process. This process clearly benefits capitalism far more than workers.

Since the 1980s capitalism has undergone a major process of restructuring in industry and services in general which has also facilitated the global restructuring of business organisation. This restructuring and globalisation has been made possible by technological improvements to the means of production by the introduction of micro-electronics and the digitalisation in computing and communication systems. These systems have made manufacturing and communications far more efficient and thrown enormous numbers out of work through the writing off of the mechanical, electrical and manual systems that were used previously.   Nevertheless, as has always happened within capitalism, new technologies such as digital, biogenetic and materials technologies also generate new products and new industries which create new jobs and new markets for capitalists.

These innovations have enabled capitalism to become more efficient by continuing to increase the productivity (ie exploitation) of workers and globalise production and service provisions.

During the last 50 years, it has also become more and more common for wage rises to be linked to further measures for improving productivity, as though this is only way that capitalism can fund increased wages. What should be evident now is that improved productivity simply tends to increase (at least until competitors catch up) the unpaid portion of labour in relation to the paid portion. So whilst workers may get what are usually small increases in wage (if inflation has not already wiped out the benefit), the capitalist tends to gain even more.

Marx called the ratio sv/v the rate of exploitation as it shows how much new surplus value is created by the working class. There is no doubt that the level of exploitation of workers during this period has increased significantly and enabled capitalism to become more efficient. This has enabled capitalism to maintain itself but nevertheless the working class still experiences austerity, social wage reductions and wage limitations imposed by the ruling class.

14   Labour and the Subsistence Wage

Ignoring mathematical formulae for a moment, if we look at the real world around us, we can see the existence of buildings, machinery, transport systems, manufactured products and even raw materials. We need to ask very simple questions about this - who owns it all and how did these assets come into being?

They are all owned to the very great majority by the ruling class, the capitalist class, but who built and constructed them? Did the capitalists? This can't possibly be true because they don't do anything other than just sit there and tell others what to do. How do all these assets come into being - by paying workers to build them. To paraphrase, the working class created them all.

So take another look at the world around you, isn't it now obvious who this system depends on. The workers that have built every single thing that exists, not the fatcats trading money and goods on the stock market!

Yet, what does the working class own? Just enough to live on and keep working!

The capitalists hold the wealth and buy labour to build new goods and then reap the benefits of the new wealth created. OK, let's be generous here, the working class earns subsistence wages but this does not mean all are living at starvation level. This value of subsistence varies across the world and some workers even earn enough to own some luxuries. In Europe, some workers earn sufficient to enjoy a reasonable standard of living in comparison to workers in Africa for example. This changes nothing about the labour process in general and the exploitation of all workers. Some ideologues still argue that western workers are privileged, that they are the workers aristocracy, even Engels wrote in such terms. However, we have established that all workers experience a process whereby a large part of the value of their labour is stolen by the ruling class; all workers are exploited no matter how much they receive as a wage.

We are also told paid labour is honest labour, but it is always a means by which the ruling class extracts surplus value from workers and leaves them with sufficient only for subsistence, in other words, it is a system for the exploitation of workers.

The amount of assets owned by workers even today, let alone in Marx's time, remains negligible compared to the assets owned by the ruling class. The wages paid to the working class are simply enough to maintain a limited lifestyle and worse, for many workers in the world, their income only means poverty and hunger.

In the 21st century, subsistence means something different to that in Marx's time. Today, in the UK , subsistence means owning a car, washing machine, cookers, as well as leisure items such as TVs, Xboxes, stereos and computers. Subsistence however means something different in different parts of the world. In the UK, for example, subsistence also includes house ownership or, more precisely, mortgages because, as mentioned previously, it is normal in the UK to purchase houses on credit to live in. In most parts of the globe it is normal to rent accommodation but in some parts workers have to build their own houses out of scrap - this hardly amounts to ownership though. Subsistence levels then are socially determined (just as described earlier for the value of wages and of labour power).

What must be recognised from a global standpoint then is that the working class stands outside the system and has no economic wealth to protect within the system. Its income is sufficient for subsistence only. To some extent this subsistence wage may enable what appear to be some luxury or leisure items but it does not allow for workers as a whole to escape their situation. Some may be able to start small businesses and become self-employed, but in today's economy this makes little difference to status, it has just become a cheaper way for employers to exploit workers. Certainly some individuals, through specific circumstances, break through this barrier and become capitalists but they are the exception.

To repeat, in general workers have no distinct role within the system other than to work and no ownership of anything substantial. Fig. 3 below shows the reality of that generalisation.

47 million people own 44% of the global wealth, just over 500 million people across the world own 83% of the wealth and 4.5 billion adults own just 17% of wealth.

In summary, wages paid to the working class are nothing but subsistence and the work they do for their employers creates an ever growing mass of buildings and manufacturing resources let alone luxuries, houses, cars and yachts for the capitalist.

Figure 3 The Global Wealth Pyramid 2019 [xi]

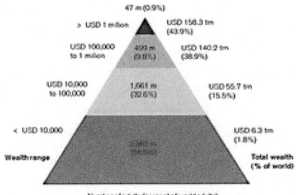

Source: James Davies, Rodrigo Lluberas and Anthony Shorrocks,
Global wealth databook 2019

15   Labour and Today's Standard of Living

There is another issue which is worth raising here and that is what is called our standard of living. We are continually told we are much better off than people in the past and clearly, there is far more value in the world than in Marx's time. Capitalism as a system has grown substantially. Does that mean workers are better off now than they were 100 or 150 years ago? Does that mean capitalism is benefitting us all?

This question is not so straightforward to answer as it may first seem.

In Europe, we all live in modernised cities with roads, public transport, services for waste disposal, energy and communications, as well as more personal possessions such as cars, Xboxes, mobile phones, computers, washing machines and other kitchen equipment and so on. This is far, far more than existed in Marx's time.

Do we take this at face value and say of course we are then better off!

Should we not also consider however that just to be able to work, social needs have increased. In the current environment, cars, phones and washing machines are essential.

Certainly there are features that represent an improvement in leisure and contribute to making tasks easier for individuals. Today however society places more demands on workers and this means we just do not have the time to waste in washing clothes by hand or in cleaning house with scrubbing brushes. Just like mobile phones and email systems bring the apparent benefit of quicker communications, they also generate not only extra costs but extra tasks and extra stress because the demands for immediate responses, both in home life and at work, are that much greater.

The complexity of needs today means that it is all too easy for working people to fall further into the poverty traps when things start to go wrong. An illness, a car crash and other accidents whether to yourself or a family member, loss of a job due to personal conflict, cost cutting on insurances, PTSD from both social and military conflict and the impact of environmental problems, etc can all start life unravelling and lay bare the tenuous grip that subsistence wages give us on life.

The point is that all people, and particularly the working class, need to purchase higher proportion of resources to survive in society, maintain their families and maintain what is the standard lifestyle. This is not being better off. This just means we need more to sustain ourselves and prevent us falling into poverty.

We also need to recognise that even in the so-called developed world, poverty and homelessness are rising and standards of living are falling as it becomes clear that growth in the world economy is slowing down and stagnation is threatened.

This section, in fact most of the pamphlet, has focussed on the UK and developed countries in general. In the poorer regions of the world there are some countries that have developed into industrial nations, but the levels of poverty still remain very high in these countries and the level of public services remains very low. The term underdeveloped is still appropriate therefore. Figure 4 below shows how the developed world has been able to grow and how for example Africa has not. Generally speaking, the international trade practices of capitalism such as the demand for cash crops by powerful companies actually prevents poorer and more dependant countries being able today to develop into an all-round society in the way that Europe and America had by the first half of the 20th Century. In the UK and other European countries we should not be blasé about how well capitalism has developed, we should not fail to remember and empathise with the dreadful conditions that our fellow workers experience in other parts of the world.

Figure 4. GDP per Capita [xii]

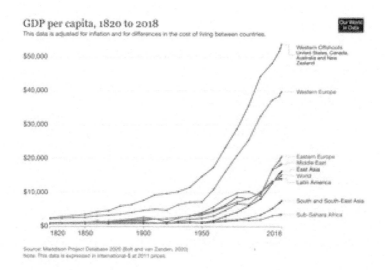

16   Unpaid Labour can be Broken Down into different elements

We have established that the labour process generates new value but when Marx used this model, he identified the value of total capital as only including capital that can be applied to the next cycle of production. Surplus value is therefore extracted from the unpaid labour of the working class but is composed only of value that contributes to new cycles of production and to the accumulation of new capital.

Marx's chapter on this topic in 'Wages, Prices and Profit' is somewhat limited. He discusses the idea that surplus value generated only goes towards 3 destinations:

"*Rent, interest, and industrial profit* are only different names for different parts of the *surplus value* of the commodity, or the *unpaid labour enclosed in it*, and they are *equally derived from this source and from this source alone*". [xiii]

Firstly we should add that the social wage is another element of unpaid labour certainly from the point of view of individual businesses and also a further element of surplus value. However as surplus value it contributes to the subsistence and reproduction of the working class not manufacturing capital, so we should see the social wage globally as a contribution to the next round of variable capital expenditure.

We should also recognise that whilst these 4 items are the entirety of surplus value, they are not the entire value of the unpaid labour. There are further costs that have to be covered out of the extra value that have been generated by workers' unpaid labour, which do not enable further value to be generated and are just used up by the ruling class and its state. This range of unproductive costs incurred by capitalism is just another burden on the working class and has greatly expanded with the growth of state capitalism in the 20th Century. Today society is formed of a complex web of systems which act as a drain on the value created by labour.

What Marx did not discuss in 'Wages Prices and Profit', probably because it was nowhere near as important as it is today, is this range of waste expenditures derived from this general pool of unpaid labour. Remember waste expenditure does not create surplus value and hence does not contribute to capital accumulated for the next phases of production.

The obvious element is the subsistence of the ruling class - although subsistence may not be the best word because they enjoy a luxurious existence. Even in Marx's day the personal income of the capitalists and their families had to be understood as a product of the unpaid labour extracted from workers and therefore part of the burden placed on workers.

Some commodity production manufactures goods that may generate profits for individual businesses, but these products do not represent any additional value for global capital in that they cannot be used in the next round of accumulation of new capital. We call these unproductive industries and the main example of this would be the armaments industry. This industry employs workers to produce goods that can be sold for a profit by individual businesses but they are either used in capitalisms' constant wars or just stored away. In terms of global capital, this is simply waste. We could also add other sectors such as large parts of the financial markets, insurance, football agents and even professional criminals (if you can call that an industry).

Marx used the example of a tailor to explain the basic difference between productive and unproductive labour. A tailor working for a business set up to provide repair services is productive as each worker creates surplus values which contributes to future growth of the business. Whereas when an individual employs a tailor directly to repair clothes, this labour is just an expense to the recipient of the service and creates no surplus value. It is therefore is an unproductive expense in global terms and a burden on global unpaid labour.

The same task may therefore be both productive and unproductive depending on how it is carried out and herein lies the complication in explaining waste production. It is to be noted here that what creates surplus value is a relationship of employer to employee rather than the actual product itself.

Some service industries are also unproductive in global terms and therefore are a drain on unpaid labour. However the analysis of service industries into productive and unproductive industries has become far more complex since Marx's time. Indeed there are many grey areas over which we can dispute eg is retail to be considered as productive because it is part of the distribution industry or is it an unproductive process of buying and selling? Does Facebook or Twitter generate new value? Frankly this task has become problematic even for specialists so providing definitive answers to this problem is well beyond the scope of this pamphlet.

What is far more important than the answers to these questions is to understand that the majority of workers (lets exclude paid management) in these businesses are nevertheless still part of the working class. Even if they do not engage in productive labour, they still have the same experience of labour and wage slavery.

It can be easy to see though that many outsourced services such as transportation, computing, cleaning, training and so forth do contribute productively to other businesses producing and hence contribute to the whole process of accumulation of capital. Indeed one reason the service sector is said to have grown so much is that the large manufacturing firms, which used to do all these tasks themselves, have been broken down into smaller specialist firms during the last couple of decades in the 20th Century. Many sections of these early large firms now function as independent service providers to the final manufacturer.

Last but not least, we should also consider here the major role of the nation state in administering society nowadays. Over the last century, national states have grown enormously in size simply because the roles they perform have grown enormously. Apart from their functions in providing a social wage to the working class and any productive manufacturing businesses they manage, all state expenditure on eg administration of legislation, foreign policy, trade policies, defence and the policing of society and so on is unproductive and is therefore another category of costs that act as a burden on the additional value generated by workers. Of particular interest to the UK in 2020 should be the role of the customs process and customs officials themselves. Globally seen these are just artificial processes that contribute nothing to the accumulation of new capital, they are just waste expenditure therefore and an extra expense for both the working class and British capital.

What Marx said is correct then, but it does not get close to explaining just how big the burden is on the working class and how big the unpaid labour extracted from the working class has become.

17   Wages and Inflation

One of the ways bourgeois society works is by blaming workers for causing its problems. Marx stated that the ruling ideology in society is always the ideology of the ruling class and this was never more clear than during the current period in terms of the way ideas, ie the press and government propaganda, are used to control workers.

It is common practice for striking workers to be blamed for causing problems for other workers. When nurses or transport workers or power workers threaten strike action to defend their own living standards, the press, the government and the employers all weigh in with their attacks about how others will be stopped from working and will be hurt or killed in some way.

One particular way in which this happens is the blaming worker for price increases. The idea of wage inflation is a hypocritical attack on workers seeking to defend themselves against austerity and trying to improve their standard of living. Capitalism in the 21st Century cannot provide improved living standards so it has to attack workers with these myths to try to keep them in check and minimise its own problems.

Figure 5. UK Inflation - The current equivalent of £1 in 1850 [xiv]

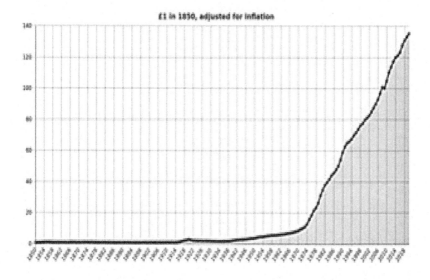

As we can see from Figure 5, UK inflation has only become a major issue since the 1970s. Does that mean that wages didn't go up before that time. No, of course it doesn't, something else went wrong with the economy from that time on to cause inflation. What the chart shows though is not annual inflation, but how the social value of the £1 has fallen in that time – frankly of far more importance to workers. It shows what a £1 in 1850 is equivalent to in money value in following years so that in 1970 it was worth £8.7 and in 2018 it is worth £133.1. Contrast this with Figure 6 which shows that the average household income has only increased by little more than twice between 1975 and 2018.

Workers are underpaid for their labour and it is the ruling class and the nation state that are responsible for inflation.

Figure 6 Average UK Household Income 2019 [xv]

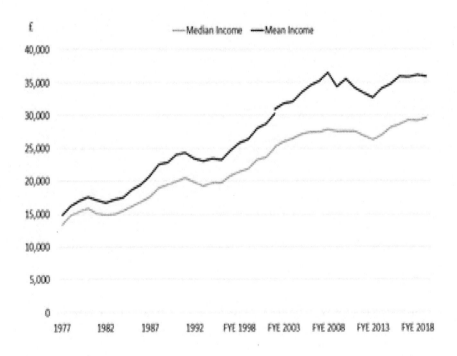

18   In Conclusion

Why concern ourselves with wage labour and exploitation?

Isn't it normal, some have money and some don't - it's always been like that!

The relationship between worker and capitalist that this pamphlet has described is the basis of class struggle. It explains strikes, strike waves and confrontations with the state and it explains the repression of workers and poor by the state apparatus. It is also the basis for how nationalism and anti-strike propaganda is being used in this first period of the 21st Century to keep workers in order and to keep capitalists making profits.

Without going into detailed history, it also helps us understand how workers in the slave society of the Romans and Greeks and in the feudal society in Europe had very different relationships with their ruling class since wage labour did not exist then. This means that it is wrong to say 'it's normal' to experience what we have today and it is wrong to think that capitalism is anything other than temporary.

The changes in capitalism since 1914 with world wars, constant regional conflicts, the growth of the state apparatus and the constant search for means to increase exploitation of the working class shows a system in decline.

In writing this conclusion, society is in the midst of the coronavirus lockdown. It is not at all clear how the journey of the virus will work itself out nor how well capitalism will survive and nor how much people will suffer.

What is absolutely clear however is how a money-based society is incapable of responding in a genuinely humane fashion. There is a real confrontation taking place between financial concerns ie the protection of the economy and the protection of businesses and industries, and the need to protect human beings from a virus which is causing a large number of deaths and making a much larger number of people across the world dangerously ill.

Capitalism has not been able to respond quickly and effectively to the health needs of the world –because money, waged labour and commodity production get in the way. Capitalism presents itself as normal, but it is the very existence of money that is causing even more disruption of everyday life (over and above the virus itself) and increasing poverty for everyone.

Socialism, genuine socialism, means a class free society without money and waged labour, private property and classes. It means a society that can work to everyone's benefit without the restraints that we have today.

Footnotes

Marx, Karl. *Value, Price and Profit*. Introductory editorial; New York: International Co., Inc, 1969;

[ii] Luxemburg, Rosa. *What is Economics?* in *Rosa Luxemburg Speaks* Pathfinder Press, 1970

[iii] estimated from a 34million working population earning an average of £26,000 pa

[iv] Marx, Karl. *Wages, Price and Profit*. New York: International Co., Inc, 1969;

[v] Marx, Karl. *Wages, Price and Profit*. New York: International Co., Inc, 1969;

[vi] Marxists Internet Archive Encyclopedia. *https://www.marxists.org/glossary/terms/l/a.htm#labour-theory-value Accessed on 29.5.20*

[vii] Our World in Data,, 2020, https://ourworldindata.org/government-spending Accessed 10.3.20

[viii] Our World in Date. 2020 - *Government Spending,* https://ourworldindata.org/government-spending Accessed 10.3.20

[ix] Economic Research Council. http://ercouncil.org/2018/chart-of-the-week-week-47/ Accessed 10.3.20

[x] Dickens C. 1850, *David Copperfield*

[xi] Credit Suisse, 2019, *Press Release Global Wealth Report 2019,* https://www.credit-suisse.com/about-us-news/en/articles/media-releases/global-wealth-report-2019--global-wealth-rises-by-2-6--driven-by-201910.html Accessed on 10.3.20

[xii] Our World in Data, 2020 https://ourworldindata.org/economic-growth, Accessed 10.3.20

[xiii] Marx, Karl. *Wages, Price and Profit*. New York: International Co., Inc, 1969;

[xiv] £1 in 1850 → 2020 | UK Inflation Calculator." Official Inflation Data, Alioth Finance, 5 Mar. 2020, https://www.officialdata.org/uk/inflation/1850?amount=1. Accessed on 10.3.20

[xv] Office of National Statistics. *Average UK Household Income 2019,* Accessed on 10.3.20 https://www.ons.gov.uk/peoplepopulationandcommunity/personalandhouseholdfinances/incomeandwealth/bulletins/householddisposableincomeandinequality/financialyearending2019